SURVIVING THE OFFICE

A SUPPORT STAFF'S GUIDE TO SUCCESS

Caroline Partridge

In accordance with the United States Copyright Act of 1976, the scanning, uploading, and electronic sharing of any part of this book without permission of the author constitutes unlawful piracy and theft of intellectual property. If you would like to use the material from the book, prior written permission must be obtained. You can contact the author via email: carolinepartridge299@gmail.com. Thank you for supporting the author and her rights.

SURVIVING THE OFFICE: A SUPPORT STAFF'S GUIDE TO SUCCESS

Cover Design: Madame Solaire Studios

All rights reserved.

First Digital Edition, October 2022

ISBN: 9798359427951 | ASIN: B0BK26T6P2

Independently Published

I would like to thank Nick Kennedy for his awesome illustrations, Katie for editing, and Brittney for the cover and the help with self-publishing. And a big thank you to all of the office staff who kindly filled out a survey. I would also like to thank every office support personnel I have ever worked with; you all have taught me a lot.

Contents

PRELUDE — 1
1. Communication — 5
2. Delegation — 12
3. Queen Bee Syndrome — 17
4. Change — 23
5. Gossip — 27
Afterword — 31
About Author — 32

PRELUDE

I used to work in a busy medical office with four support staff. One of our support staff, Jane, often interjected into people's conversations with helpful advice, which I found useful as I was in the learning stage. But her interjections annoyed my other coworkers. Jane had a tendency to condescend when talking on the telephone and to her coworkers. That's it. In my opinion, she was very tolerable. However, my two other coworkers did not like her–at all. Jane came in later than us and there was a good hour of opportunity to converse without her presence. And boy, did they converse. Every morning I would hear gossip such as "she is a miserable person." She did this horrible thing and that awful thing. Then when Jane came in, my coworkers' demeanors towards her changed to bright and bubbly. You would think they were all best friends. My two other coworkers were participating in pretty bad gossip behind Jane's back, but were extremely pleasant to her in person. I thought that if my coworkers were talking about her behind her back, they were probably talking about me behind my back too, as I was the newbie making all the mistakes. Once there was a mistake made by two of us that resulted in grave ramifications. My three coworkers waited until I left and then gossiped about the situation with the nurse practitioner and decided I was fully to blame. The nurse practitioner had some words with me the next day. I asked for a meeting with all of us so I could present my side of the story. "There is not going to be a meeting," said one of my coworkers. Wow! So when I was telling everyone at the practice that I had given my notice to make more money, one physician said, "I know they're not the friendliest bunch." What did she mean by that? Were they gossiping about me in my absence as well?

Fast forward a year. Linda was great to work with. She taught me about insurance verification and did so with grace. If you are able to not only verify insurance but obtain authorizations as well, your worth to the company increases, as does your job security. Linda willingly shared all of her knowledge and helped me immensely, without reserve. One of our tasks was to bring the shredding buckets downstairs to the large shredding container. When I hurt my knee, Linda happily did my share of this task. Not only was Linda concerned for the welfare of her coworkers, but she altruistically helped them. She was also very helpful to our other coworker as well.

There are many factors of office behavior that can make you love or hate your job, and after working as an office support staff for over 30 years, I think I have experienced almost everything.

This guide discusses the factors behind such office issues as communication style, delegating, the queen bee syndrome, change, and gossip, which, depending on how they are handled, can make or break an office job. These issues are not often discussed during job interviews, nor are commonly found in job descriptions. In my 32 years of office support experience, I have been entangled in these issues and have thought a lot about how to handle them in the best way. Who wants to be miserable at work because of issues not often discussed but are very much present in support jobs? Survey results from office support staff are discussed at the end of each section. Without further delay, let's get started.

Chapter One

Communication

Communication

WHICH WAY DO YOU SAY?

There are many means of communication: email, paid courier (i.e., US postal), telephone, fax, and interpersonal contact, to name a few. There are different personality styles of the communicator and receptor: quiet at one end of the continuum, bold and forthright at the other end, and somewhere in between. Other factors come into play, such as time, the physical distance between you and the receiving party, and the need to reach several people at once with your message. Are we communicating with someone internally or outside of our organization? Are there any pitfalls to any communication methods? With these competing factors, how do we decide to use which means of communication at work?

The personality-style-driven approach chooses communication consistent with the communicators' or receptor's level of ease. "I don't want to interrupt this person, so I will send an email." Or, "I need to have a personal interaction with opportunity for face-to-face discussion" says the next person. This type of decision making will suit yourself but possibly not others. I have found over the years that the receiving party's needs are more important than mine if I want my message to have a good reception. So rather than focus on my preferences, I think about that of the receptors. Would Ann prefer an email or a visit by me to her office? Does my supervisor prefer email or face-to-face? At first, we don't always know, so answering this question may take some trial and error or asking people of their preferences. Once I have a good feel for one's receptive preferences, I will use that method with him or her. This leads to effectively transmitting your message because of good reception.

Distance and time are important. If Robert is in a separate building that is a 15-minute walk from my office, then an email or a phone call would be best. That is just common sense logic. We are usually too busy to use one-half hour of travel time to communicate one issue with one person. If the distance is great between me and the receptor, and he or she prefers an interpersonal method, then the telephone is the best choice. Regardless of the receptor's preferences, I am sure that he or she will understand that the distance between us warrants a phone call.

Time and multiple recipients can contribute to the communication choice. Sometimes you need to communicate with more than one person on one issue. My issue is with Nancy, but

I think my supervisor should be in the loop, so I will communicate with him at the same time. Does this communication deserve a meeting? Again, time consumption comes into play. We all do not have time to have a meeting on every issue involving two or more people. I may need to tell someone of a policy my supervisor wrote and let him know I was quoting him. But a meeting is unnecessary. In this situation, an email to all involved is a choice that fits well.

I have to communicate with someone outside of our facility. Do I fax, email, call, or mail? If the communication needs to be documented, then calling is eliminated. If it is confidential information, then faxing should be eliminated as almost anyone can pick documents off of a fax machine at the receiving end. If it is regarding a facility client, then one may want to avoid email due to internet security issues. Therefore, in this case, documentation, confidentiality, and security are the driving factors for me to choose US Postal mail.

Faxing and emailing are methods of choice when time is a factor. Does the parent need the report for tomorrow's meeting with the school?

Then we should fax or email it consistent with company policies.

Emails can sometimes be a pitfall; therefore, my preference, holding all other factors equal, is interpersonal communication. Often, emails can be perceived as negative when it was meant to be concise. With interpersonal communication, we have positive body language, including smiling, to help transmit our message in a positive way. If you don't understand fully what the other is saying, you are right there to clarify it with several to-and-fro interactions. There is no misunderstanding emotional content. There is no misunderstanding the message. And socialization occurred as well.

As you can see, this is not just about what particular situations warrant faxing, emailing, paid courier, phone call, or interpersonal interaction, but rather it is about a myriad of interacting factors, each of which need to weigh in on the decision. For example, if I need to communicate with someone a car ride away, and she does not answer emails or phone calls regularly, I may decide to pay a personal visit even though the traveling time factor warrants otherwise. Or I may know that my supervisor prefers to communicate personally, but my sprained ankle is keeping me fairly stationary, then an email or phone call will need to be the choice. In a prior medical records position, we preferred to use paid courier (US Postal) to send protected health information as it is the securest way to reach a recipient. However, we will fax to the emergency room as emergent factors override other factors. The weight we place on each factor is a bit different for all of us.

Of 28 reporting of how they most often communicate inside of their office, 57% most often use interpersonal communication while 14% most often use email and 29% most often use telephone. Of 26 reporting of how they communicate outside of the office, 12% most often use email, and 85% most often used telephone to communicate, and 4% most often used fax. Not one of the respondents most often used US mail.

LEADING QUESTIONS:

1. How do you communicate?

2. Is your communication method different with different people?

What communication factors weigh in most heavily with you?

Chapter Two

Delegation

Delegation

SHOULD WE LOVE OR HATE TO DELEGATE?

We all hate when someone else does one of our tasks poorly. Really, that someone does not do it right. Now that step that is not done right will affect a future step and mess that step up, too. Heck, now the whole process is in jeopardy. "I should have just done it myself," we say as we struggle to get our work completed.

We all love it when we have a cumbersome task that seems like it will never be completed, and a helpful coworker offers to help and get a significant part done quickly. "Now I can meet my deadline. Now a huge burden is lifted."

So which is it? Do you love or hate to delegate?

Let's look at the pros and cons of each scenario. When you hate to delegate and opt to do everything yourself, things get done right. You do not have to repeat the work of a less knowledgeable helper, nor do you have to spend time training. Other steps in the process will go smoothly. Negative fallouts from errors are less likely to occur. You can rest easy. Except that it took you so long to do everything that your desk is a mess, your mind is in a tizzy, and you feel pressure to get work done in a time frame that is too narrow.

But the next time you did, delegate. That helpful coworker took on your scanning job on the dedicated scanner and completed it in half an hour that would have otherwise taken you hours to do at the copier/scanner as you planned. You can tell your supervisor that the project is done already. Your supervisor will be pleased. You have more time to tackle those other projects on the back burner. But what if the helpful coworker, not knowing what you know about the specifics of the project, makes a mistake that will come back to haunt you later as the mistake will affect other steps in the process? "If only the coworker knew what I know, then the mistake would not have happened. Maybe I should have done this myself."

We cannot make a decision yet on whether or not to delegate based on the above examples. We need to qualify and quantify the chance of error of delegating: Does this chance of error outweigh the benefit of getting a cumbersome task done quickly by a helper? We need to brainstorm what the potential errors are. What could happen as a result of a mistake in this or that part of the project? Once you have done this, a simple risk assessment will help here. What is the likelihood of a potential mistake happening often? What is the likelihood that the potential mistake will cause grave ramifications? If the occurrence of a potential error is great, if the ramification of potential error is great, or both, then you may want to do this yourself or train the helper. If the opposite is true, that the potential error is not likely to occur often, or the ramifications of the mistake are mild, it is time to delegate.

We cannot do every task ourselves. That unfortunate person ends up with a messy desk, fatigue, and complaints about the workload. However, if a mistake is likely to occur often or with great, negative ramifications, it would behoove you to be able to say you did train the helper. Or you could have done it yourself.

It sometimes takes a degree of letting go, of stepping off the edge of security to delegate. But if you train correctly, and do not anticipate large numbers of or serious errors, then it can also be a moment of liberation.

Of 26 reporting if they like to have a coworker help them with a cumbersome task, 58% said yes, 42% said sometimes, and 0% said no.

LEADING QUESTIONS:

1. Give two reasons why it would be good to have a coworker help you with a cumbersome task.

2. Give a situation in which it could not be beneficial to have a coworker help you with a cumbersome task.

Chapter Three

Queen Bee Syndrome

How to Avoid Queen Bee Syndrome

HOW TO AVOID THE QUEEN BEE SYNDROME

We know what "Queen Bee" refers to: It is the person in the office who wants to be in unofficial control, the non-management person everyone goes to with questions, the person without whom the office could not possibly run. She is always complaining that she has too much work to do and never finishes things because she thinks "if I don't do it, it will not get done right." This can result in her unofficially delegating menial tasks so she can finish the complicated ones. The end result: A person who is bossy without being the boss. We have all run into this person. One thing we never imagine is that this person would be ourselves!

Avoiding being a Queen Bee is fairly simple. Instead of avoiding pitfalls mentioned above, take these positive steps in working well with others:

1. **Be genuinely altruistic and concerned for the welfare and happiness of your coworkers.** If you want your coworkers to be happy and content at their job, then you will be more apt to listen and encourage them and not try to unofficially supervise them.   A little concern in the office goes a long way. For example, if one coworker is having difficulty keeping to her usual work schedule due to family reasons, it is

good to support her getting permission to change her hours. If she is happier, everyone else in the office will be happier too. Or if she wants to take some classes to advance her position at work, encourage her, and use your skills to help her if needed. Once a work partner wanted to get a degree but was apprehensive about writing with which I offered to help. It is a win/win here for both parties.

2. **Be democratic.** One way to do this is to view the office as a partnership or co-op of people who all contribute and decide upon things equally. Of course you need to follow your supervisor's instructions, but for situations that do not need supervisory involvement, then have a discussion and decide on it together. Brainstorm the reasons why a choice would be good and bad, and together, make a logical choice that is based on potential outcomes not on doing it "my way because I have always done it that way." This democratic discussion of the pros and cons will make the

implementation of the decision easier as we now have reasons why we are doing something a certain way; the decision will become more meaningful and easier to implement because now we know "why." The democratic discussion also instills feelings or worth and the resulting decisions will positively affect the company. It is fulfilling to think we are helping the company (and ourselves) by preprinting labels to save ourselves time later.

3. **Be organized.** Spending a minute of organizational time now can really save you an hour later. If you find ways to complete tasks quicker without sacrificing quality, you will not be that person who has so much on his plate that he feels the need to delegate unofficially to others. For example, will a form letter suffice in this situation? Will the receiving party of the form letter be unhappy that it was not a personally drawn-up letter? What is the worst that can happen with this form letter? If you weigh the possible outcomes with the

time savings, you may find that the form letter, saving you about 3 hours per week, is worth any potential risk. Do you have a task with many steps and forget what steps have been accomplished? Do you need a task tracker? Should it be in paper or computer format? Spending a minute tracking tasks has always saved me time in the long run and kept the effectiveness of the project at a high level. I don't ever feel the need to delegate to my coworkers to do this or that due to having too much on my plate.

In short, none of us wants to be the queen bee nor be around one. By being altruistic, democratic, and organized, we can avoid this pitfall in ourselves and produce a happier work atmosphere as well.

Of 25 reporting, 60% said they have a person in their office who is bossy without being the boss, and 40% say they do not.

LEADING QUESTIONS:

1. Give one way you could use to keep from being a "queen bee" at the office.

2. How do you feel when a non-supervisory peer issues a directive rather than discusses it with the team? How likely are you to adhere to this directive?

Chapter Four

Change

Change

EMBRACING CHANGE

If you hear yourself saying "This is the way we have always done it," then this discussion is for you. I'd rather say, "Why am I doing it this way"? Is my method due to 1) law, 2) company policy, 3) industry standard, 4) risk assessment, or 5) at your supervisor's request? These are all sound reasons for a procedure. There are other good reasons, of course, such as the procedure works very well for the task at hand. But for now, we will focus on the above 5. "This is the way we have always done it" is not a sound reason. If the reason does not fit into one of the 5 categories above, you may want to review. Change may be warranted.

One way to embrace change is to encourage others to share their ideas. The tried-and-true practice of brainstorming can be useful. Are you together physically? Write down all responses to the query posed regardless of how relevant you may think they are. After this phase, the group will pick out the most efficacious ideas on which to concentrate. This way, all will have contributed and feel involved, which in turn, will make the changes easier to implement, thus embracing change.

Show your enthusiasm for change; it may be contagious. A positive verbal or written response can go a long way. If a colleague poses a new procedure, discuss its merits and thank the colleague for proposing. You do not have to agree with this new procedure to do this. If change does result from this proposal, it will help all involved to think positively about it.

Do a risk assessment by looking at the qualitative and quantitative effects of a possible error of the task. If an error is highly likely to occur (quantitative), then proactive measures should be taken to avoid the error – thus change. If the error could produce highly undesirable effects (qualitative), then again, proactive measures should be taken to avoid the error – again change. If both types of errors could occur, then you definitely need some proactive measures, which are change; and in these cases, change is good.

These are some ways to embrace change. Some procedures we may not want to change, such as those based on law, policy, industry standard, risk analysis, or per supervisor. But for procedures that do not fall into these categories, thinking about the "whys" and then better ways to accomplish the procedure are fruitful and fun.

Of 24 reporting, 33% embrace change at work, 46% are a bit leery of it, and 21% are not a big fan.

LEADING QUESTIONS:

1. Name a recent office change and how you handled it.

2. Discuss a situation in which an office change went well for you.

Chapter Five

Gossip

Gossip

D **ID YOU HEAR?**

Gossip. A bad four-letter, er... six-letter word. Most know it is to be avoided, and that it causes harm. Just what kind of harm does it cause? Who is affected? How does it make people feel?

While most know to avoid gossip, we all have probably participated in it at some point. On a past occasion, I thought that when a disgruntled employee suddenly took time off, such as a day here and a day there, that this employee was looking for new employment. I was tempted to tell a coworker my prediction to see if I would be proven right, and then she would know how clever I was.

What would happen if I told a coworker that I thought another coworker was looking for a new job? Take, for example, an imaginary office. I feel that Samantha is looking for a new job so I whisper this to Jennifer. Jennifer may think that if I am talking about Samantha to her, that I could easily talk about her (Jennifer) to others. Jennifer may feel uncomfortable sharing a secret about Samantha with whom she is friendly.

In order to share this gossip, I lower my voice to a whisper. Sam, who works nearby, overhears me whispering something and wonders if I am talking about him. Similarly, Sam may wonder why I did not share the secret with him as well and may feel left out.

I could slip and mention the gossip out loud one day, and Samantha could hear and figure out I am gossiping about her. Samantha could feel betrayed and hurt. My supervisor could overhear my gossip and remember to incorporate this negative behavior into my next evaluation.

I also could get a reputation as a gossiper. People may stay away from me, and my social contacts at work may be few. I could develop a poor self-image for behaving badly or not having friends at work.

All of these scenarios may not happen, but some could. What a mess. Better to keep my mouth shut.

Of 25 reporting, 80% said gossip occurs in their office, and 20% said gossip does not occur in their office. Of the 19 reporting that gossip does occur in their office, 32% said gossip does not bother them at all, 58% said it bothers them a little, and 11% says gossip bothers them a lot.

LEADING QUESTIONS:

1. Have you ever participated in gossip? What were the consequences?

2. Has anyone ever gossiped about you? How did that make you feel?

Afterword

Thank you for reading <u>Surviving the Office</u>. I hope this guide can help you enjoy your office job and make good decisions on the office issues mentioned.

About Author

Caroline has a Bachelor of Arts from The University of Massachusetts at Boston. She resides in the rural town of Wilton, NH with her fiance, Pete, two sons and two cats, whom she adores.

Made in the USA
Columbia, SC
22 April 2025